THE LEAVING KIND

The Leaving Kind

Tyler Tirtle

First Edition, 2025
Published by Staten House
Printed in the United States of America

ISBN: 979-8-89860-388-5

Cover and interior design by Thistle & Thread

Introduction

In 2023, a large medical study found that 11.6% of marriages end in divorce or separation when one partner faces a serious illness—mirroring general population rates. Yet when the patient is a woman, that number jumps to 20.8%, more than six times the 2.9% rate seen when the patient is a man.

This isn't a case study. It's a story.

The Leaving Kind maps the final chapter of a woman's life through poetry: a terminal diagnosis, a dissolving marriage, and the disappearance of those who couldn't stay. Her voice is raw, reflective, and sometimes resigned—a first-person account of not only physical decline, but of emotional betrayal, spiritual dissonance, and the empty space where care should have been.

The collection is organized into five movements, each capturing a stage of her unraveling. There are no recoveries here. No reconciliations. Only the accumulating weight of being left behind, and the courage it takes to keep moving forward.

What you are about to read is not fiction. It is poetic, but it is not embellished. Every word was written to honor the women who die quietly—whose grief is never mourned, whose good-byes never come.

Stay until the end. That is all it asks of you.

I

five syllables

it doesn't feel like enough
to ruin a life.

just five syllables.
two words
that sound soft,
like they would heal,
not destroy.

the doctor said it gently,
practiced, rehearsed, experienced.

i stared at the acoustic tile above his head
and counted the holes
because it was easier
than counting what i had left.

early detection

they said we caught it early—
like it would save me from
becoming a burden.

like the word early
could soften the shape
of the coffin that's coming.

the news hit like a crash
in slow motion—
time stood still,
the doctor's mouth kept moving—
statistics, percentages, treatment plans,
all of it sounding underwater.

your grip loosened,
your stare went blank,
your body still beside mine
while something essential in you
left the room.

you ghosted through the walls after that.
opened cabinets. folded laundry.
answered questions i never asked.
slept facing the edge of the bed
like you were already practicing
life without me.

you weren't in your body.
i don't blame you—
your talent for disappearing
always arrived before your tenderness.

while i asked the doctor
how much time i had left,
you asked about insurance.
about leave from work.
about logistics.

i watched you become practical
in real time,
watched love drain from your face
and reorganize itself
into obligation.

the drive home was silent.
not even music from our playlist
filled the space growing
between us.

every passing car,
every passing stranger
all belonged to the world
i was already being escorted out of.
i kept looking at your hands,
waiting for them to reach for me—
but they stayed fixed
at ten and two,

steady as a getaway driver's.

when we got home
you cleaned the kitchen
for two straight hours.
i stood there in the doorway
holding pamphlets with words like
survival rate
and treatment options,
while you avoided looking at me
like eye contact itself
might make this contagious.

that was the first night
i understood
how illness can strip a woman
down to her least lovable parts—
not the baldness,
not the vomiting,
not the scar tissue—

but the need.

cancer

chemotherapy melts your skin,
changes your insides.

and yet,
i wasn't afraid.
not until you
looked away so easily.
not until you,
disappeared
like steam from a shower
we used to share.

how you watched me wither,
and did nothing but blink.

she thinks it's treatable,
through faith,
through prayer,
through *His* hands
and their medicine.

i don't have the heart to say
i haven't believed in *Him*
since i was a little girl—
i don't have the heart to say,
it's going to *kill* me.

what parent wants to hear that?

i would rather carry my own death
in restless silence
so she can sleep.

she clasps her hands,
begins a *pater noster*,
as a tear falls down my cheek—
weeping for the woman
who will soon bury her babe.

she always called me her *miracle*.

what am i now?

the waiting room plays classical music

vivaldi played overhead,
as my body betrayed me in silence.
nurses shuffle down corridors
in bright blues, pinks, purples—
uniformed, much like the T-cells
ransacking my body.

buzzers and beepers chime,
doors open and last names are called,
dying sure is a busy business—
or through their lens,
saving lives.

minutes drag on here,
as if this room is a timeless void—
a place where hope slowly dies.

they call my name.
i stand,
as if walking towards a different answer,
a different outcome.

II

the disappearing

he started locking the door

he never used to lock it,
now even brushing his teeth is private.

his hands forgot my shape,
he handles me like i'm fragile,
like one wrong move,
and i'll fall apart.

when i used to be sick,
he would bring me soup,
run his fingers through my hair—
he would take care of me,
like i always did for him.

but now,
i throw up violently,
no one holding my hair back.

he's out *working*,
or so he says.

i am breaking in more ways,
coming undone from my core,
an unraveling
he can't bear to witness.

he hides in his office.
he buries himself in work.
he takes on case after case—

all in an effort to avoid watching
me die slowly.

refrigerator light

you became a ghost
i only saw at night
bathed in that blue-light;
how you used to curse the kids
for how much they stared at that device.

you never knew i watched,
curled up in agony,
biting my lip until it bled,
grief carved quiet rivers
as you *shopped.*

not for food,
not for comfort,
just something newer,
unopened,
easier to swallow,
not sick,
not going to die—

s o o n .

we barely say *i love you*
but we still reach for each other
before we fall asleep—
a habit neither of us
has thought to break yet.

we don't talk the way we used to.
we used to talk about everything—
our younger years, our smaller dreams,
the old couple we swore we'd never become.

he doesn't play our song anymore.

we passed the place we had our first kiss
on the way to my treatment—
the one he always pointed out
with that cheesy grin he had
when we first met.

he didn't say anything.
neither did i.

we barely say *i love you*—
and i wonder if he still means it
when he doesn't.

the dog still sleeps on his side of the bed

he doesn't sleep here anymore,
but the dog still does—
at least he is still loyal.

it started with staying out late,
then weekends,
then weeks at a time.

before i knew it,
your things started to disappear.
one drawer at a time,
you vanished.

i begged and pleaded.
i apologized for getting sick,
i swore to you i would take care of myself—
you didn't have to do anything.
just please,
don't leave me.

your mother told me
you were talking about divorcing me.

why?

is me dying,
not final enough?

day forty-one, or maybe forty-two—
the days have stopped
being different from each other.

i've been writing to you.
in a notebook you'll probably never find,
tucked behind the good towels
we never use.

i don't know why i hide it.
you're never home long enough
to look for anything.

i write about the small things—
the way the dog moves
to your side of the bed each night
like he's still waiting.

the way i've stopped
cooking for two
but keep setting out two plates.

the way i said fine
to my mother again today
because the truth takes more
than i have left to spend.

i write about you, too.
more than i should.

more than you deserve.

if you find this after—
and you might, you might—

would you cry?
would you miss me?
would you care?

i keep writing like the answer
might change.

III

the discovery

suspicion

i saw her jogging towards the café—
the one you used to take me to every morning,
before.

something about her smile
reminded me of being in love.
reminded me of who i used to be.

i followed her inside.

she was sitting across from you
at our table.
the same one. always the same one.

i stood in the doorway long enough
to watch you look up,
find my eyes,
and go back to her
like i was nobody.

hi honey, who's this?

the bile was already in my throat
when you said it—
she's a client from work.

casual, unbothered,
like i hadn't just watched you
look at her the way

you used to look at me.

i shook her hand.
i said *it's a pleasure to meet you.*

i meant:
i know exactly what this is.
i meant:
our fucking table.
i meant:
i am dying
and you are already
replacing me.

i walked back to the car
and sat there
until the feeling passed.

it didn't pass.

will you stay with me?

i remember holding his hand
like it was a lifeline,
keeping my feet
anchored to the earth.

but the way he looked—
he looked as if i were
drowning him,
sucking the life out of him.

a fire stitched inside me
kept getting worse,
the medicines multiplied
side effects dictated everything.

i begged him.
"please, stop vanishing. i need you,"
he couldn't even look me in the eye.

he stood up.
grabbed his keys, his coat,
looked at me in my nightgown—
sweat-stained, disheveled,
and for the first time,
he spoke the truth:

"i can't do this anymore."
(he meant it.)

IV

the collapse

he didn't leave a note

the closet was half-empty.
his keys were gone.
one foot in,
the other out.

memories replay
like a broken record—
taunting me
with what was,
what should've been,
what never will be.

we promised each other forever.
my body betraying me
was not a betrayal
of my promise to you.

i stopped checking the garage
to see if his car was even in there.
i stopped caring if he was gone,
because even when he was around—
he was checked out.

and to be honest,
so am *i*.

he didn't pack everything—
just enough to tell me
he wasn't coming back.

there was no goodbye.
no note.
no "i'm sorry."

i had everything,
i had it all,
and in a matter of months,
it slipped through my fingers.

i began to yearn for the ending—
agony in my bones,
the kind that doesn't just ache
it hollows.

at first it was absence.
no keys, no music,
no garlic blooming in the air—
just stillness.

a new kind of silence.

but it echoed.
when i collapsed
down the stairs.

no one checked on me

i laid at the bottom of the stairs for hours,
waiting for someone who would never come.

too weak to move,
too tired to cry out,
i stared at the ceiling
and began to pray—
not to a god,
but for my death—
the end of this pain.

my poor child,
what an unbearable sight to behold:
her mother contorted,
broken on the floor.

how i wish she could have been spared.
how i wish i could have been spared.

several plaster casts later,
a brand new set of wheels,
and a shiny tan bracelet
with a button on it—
the kind we used to scoff at
until it became mine.

V

the dying

the machines

when the visitors go home,
the machines start to whisper here.
a gentle lull of beeps,
a whirl of liquid through a tube,
and euphoria—
or maybe a forgetting.

my body goes warm.
tingles in my hands and feet.
the burning.
the aching.
the deep agony.
slows to a halt.

it's hard for them to see me
hooked up to these machines,
tubes interlaced with my flesh,
pallid tone,
thinning cheeks,
chapped lips—
a body turned ruin, slowly.

it's been awhile
since their last visit
and i don't mind.

i don't want them to see me
decay into nothingness.

i want them to remember me
for how i was when i was alive—
not as this shell.

"happiness is a warm gun,"
paul and john would sing.

now i understood the reference
as the hospice
increased the dosage.

the morphine

the drip moves steady beside me,
a metronome ticking toward nothing.
i forget what day it is—
actually,
i forget what time feels like.

the pain fades,
but so does everything else.

memories once sharp,
now jagged glass that cut
when i try to hold on to something.

faces blur past me.
sounds blend together.
the walls melt into themselves.
i can hear my hair growing.

who am i?

where am i?
where are my kids?
where is my husband?
what —

i died the way i lived at the end—
quietly, inconveniently, and alone.

they found me in the morning,
but i had been gone for hours.
the nurse said it looked peaceful—
as if absence could be soft.
as if silence wasn't violent.

as if dying alone
wasn't its own kind of scream.

there was no one holding my hand,
no one was whispering a prayer.

i had hoped maybe he—
remembered his vow,
"in sickness and in health,"
and he would hold my hand one last time,
he would look me in the eye
and tell me how sorry he was.

and i would let go
believing him.

epilogue

While Packing

Alone in the absence of pretending, the cul-de-sac was quiet like it had known something was missing from it. A cardinal flew overhead, landing in a tree across the street. I pace the porch, counting every fastener while the seconds drained the hour dry. The roar of his 307 as it made its way through the labyrinth of asphalt and concrete interrupted the bittersweet stillness of goodbye.

He pulled up with the window down, music on, her in the passenger seat with her elbow resting on the door the way you do when you have nowhere urgent to be. He didn't cut the engine. He honked once, short and casual, while he leaned back and watched me carry boxes to the curb. He didn't come inside. He didn't offer. He stood at the end of the driveway with his hands in his pockets and for once, I didn't have the energy to hate him out loud. I had been doing that for years already and it never changed anything.

The last box I handed him was light—miscellaneous things from the hall closet. He didn't bother checking what was in it, tossed it in the back seat, and that was it. He said take care of yourself the way people say it when they mean I'm done taking care of you. I watched as he backed out of the driveway the same way he backed out of his commitment.

The notebook was small. Spiral-bound, the cover worn from being handled. I sat down on the floor of the hallway and I read it. She had written about the dog. She had written about lying to her mom because honesty was expensive and she was overdrawn on truth. She had written about him—more than you deserve, she'd said, and she was right, and she had known it, and she kept writing anyway, which is the most honest thing I have ever witnessed.

At the bottom of one page, in her handwriting where the pen had barely grazed the paper, not so much as drifting, but sloping downward toward the bottom corner of the page: would you cry?

I pressed my hand flat against the page.

He would not find this. He hadn't even come inside.

You stayed.

This book asked one thing of you at the start—stay until the end, and you did. You sat with her through the diagnosis, through the slow disappearing, through the discovery and the collapse and the dying. You were there when the machines whispered and the morphine blurred the walls. You were there in the morning.

He wasn't. But you were.

That matters more than this book can say.

She is not one woman. She is a pattern—one that repeats in hospital waiting rooms and empty beds and kitchens where someone keeps setting out two plates. The study cited in the introduction is real. But statistics don't tell you what it sounds like when a door starts getting locked that never used to be. They don't tell you what it costs to apologize for getting sick.

Poetry can't fix that. But it can be witness to it. And sometimes being witnessed is the only thing that makes the weight bearable.

You held it. You made it to the end.

That is the whole point.

—Tyler

If you or someone you love is navigating a serious illness, caregiver-abandonment, or end-of-life care, the following organizations offer support:

CancerCare — cancercare.org — free counseling, support groups, and financial assistance for people affected by cancer.

Caregiver Action Network — caregiveraction.org — resources and community for family caregivers.

National Hospice and Palliative Care Organization — nhpco.org — guidance on end-of-life care and patient rights.

Thistle & Thread Press

Neillsville, Wisconsin

Est. MMXXV